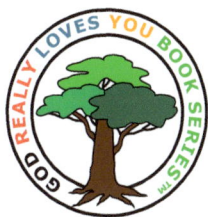

The God Really Loves You Book Series™ Presents:

GOD
Really
Loves You
and
He Hears
Your Prayers!

**Written and Illustrated
by Wendy Nelson**

God Really Loves You Book Series™ presents:

GOD Really Loves You
and He Hears Your Prayers!

Text Copyright ©2021 by Wendy Nelson
Artwork Copyright ©2021 by Wendy Nelson

Published by MediaTek Grafx
POB 62, Bonnieville, Kentucky, 42713

ISBN 978-1-0879-6073-9

Design and production by MediaTek Grafx, Bonnieville, Kentucky.

The Publisher has made every effort to avoid errors or omissions. Opinions, stories, and themes are intended for entertainment, motivation for research and future study. This book includes content that is non-fiction.

Printed in the United States of America

A Special Gift for

_____

From

_____

Note

_____

_____

_____

Date

_____

God is our Father in Heaven.
He cares about you!

God spoke to men,
so they could write
God's words down.

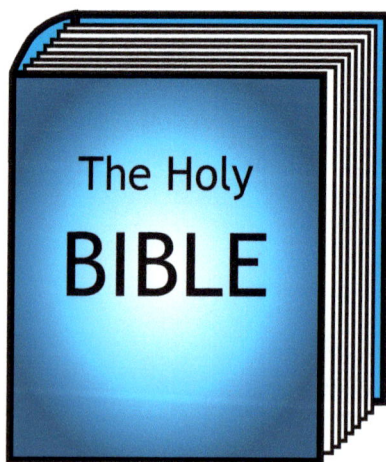

The Holy
BIBLE

A special book
called the Bible
was created to help us.

*2 Timothy 3:16-17 All scripture is given by inspiration
of God, and is profitable for doctrine, for reproof,
for correction, for instruction in righteousness:
17 That the man of God may be perfect,
thoroughly furnished unto all good works.*

The Bible
tells us to pray.

Praying
means you are
talking to God!
Wow!

We can pray about
everything!

You can pray
when you wake up.

You can pray
when you go to bed.

*1 Thessalonians 5:16-18 Rejoice evermore. 17 Pray
without ceasing. 18 In every thing give thanks: for this
is the will of God in Christ Jesus concerning you.*

God loves us and wants us to talk to Him!
God wants to hear you pray!

He loves everyone
very much!

He loves you this much!

This much
is a whole bunch!

*Psalms 17:6 I have called upon thee,
for thou wilt hear me, O God: incline thine ear unto
me, and hear my speech.
Jeremiah 29:12 Then shall ye call upon me, and ye
shall go and pray unto me, and I will hearken unto you.*

You can talk to God anytime!
You don't have to do anything special, to pray.

Many people
get down
on their knees, first.

It shows respect
to God.

Then, people
put their hands
together like this!

Sometimes,
people close their eyes,
too.

We can pray
with mommy!

We can pray
with daddy!

You can pray all by yourself!

You can talk to God all by yourself,
because He loves you!

*2 Chronicles 7:14 If my people, which are called by
my name, shall humble themselves, and pray,
and seek my face, and turn from their wicked ways;
then will I hear from heaven, and will forgive their sin,
and will heal their land.*

What do you want to pray about?

We can pray to our Father in Heaven
for many reasons!

We can thank God for nice things!

Thank you, God,
for the
pretty flowers
we smelled today!

Thank you, God,
for the purple
lizard we saw
today!

Thank you, God,
for the food we ate today!

Philippians 4:6 Be careful for nothing; but in every thing by prayer and supplication with thanksgiving let your requests be made known unto God.
Colossians 4:2 Continue in prayer, and watch in the same with thanksgiving;

We can ask God for something.

We could ask for food.

We could ask God
for the
sun to shine,
or to see
someone we love!

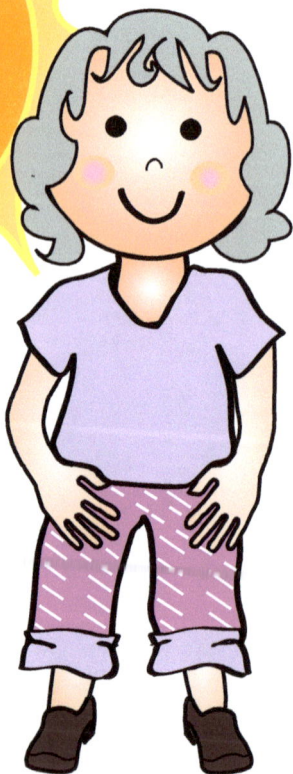

We could ask
for a new ball!

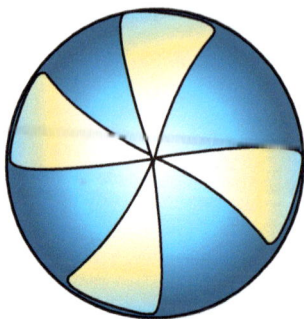

1 John 5:14 And this is the confidence that we have in him, that, if we ask any thing according to his will, he heareth us:
Matthew 21:22 And all things, whatsoever ye shall ask in prayer, believing, ye shall receive.

We can tell God whatever we want.

We can tell our Father in Heaven
that we are lonely, sad or happy.

We can tell God that we love Him!
We can tell God that we had
a really great day!

*James 5:13 Is any among you afflicted? let him pray.
Is any merry? let him sing psalms.
Psalms 4:1 Hear me when I call, O God of my
righteousness: thou hast enlarged me when I was in
distress; have mercy upon me, and hear my prayer.*

We can pray when we are scared,
or bad things happen.
We can pray if we feel sick,
and need God to make us feel better!

God will listen.

Tomorrow is a new day,
and good things will happen.
We can find good things everywhere!

*James 5:15 And the prayer of faith shall save the sick,
and the Lord shall raise him up;
Lamentations 3:22-24 It is of the LORD's mercies that
we are not consumed, because his compassions fail not.
23 They are new every morning: great is thy faithfulness.*

We can pray to God for our
brothers or sisters!

We can pray for our mommy
or daddy!

We can pray to our Father in Heaven
for our family, our neighbors and our friends!

Matthew 22:37-39 Jesus said unto him, Thou shalt love the Lord thy God with all thy heart, and with all thy soul, and with all thy mind. 38 This is the first and great commandment. 39 And the second is like unto it, Thou shalt love thy neighbour as thyself.

When we pray, God listens.
God does not always answer right away.
Sometimes, we have to wait
for the answer.

After we pray,
we listen
for the answer.
We have ears
that hear.

After we pray,
wc look
for the answer.
We have eyes
that see.

*Ezekiel 12:2 Son of man, thou dwellest
in the midst of a rebellious house,
which have eyes to see, and see not;
they have ears to hear, and hear not:
for they are a rebellious house.*

When we pray for something,
our Father in Heaven will say yes
or He will say no.
No matter what the answer is,
God loves us very much.

*Ecclesiastes 3:1 To every thing there is a season, and
a time to every purpose under the heaven:
Proverbs 3:5-6 Trust in the LORD with all thine heart;
and lean not unto thine own understanding. 6 In all thy
ways acknowledge him, and he shall direct thy paths.*

God wants you talk to Him and to love Him
more and more, as you grow up!

*Proverbs 22:6 Train up a child in the way he should
go: and when he is old, he will not depart from it.
Ephesians 6:4 And, ye fathers, provoke not
your children to wrath: but bring them up
in the nurture and admonition of the Lord.*

God really loves you and you can pray!
You can talk to your Father in Heaven,
and He hears your prayers.

GOD'S LOVE

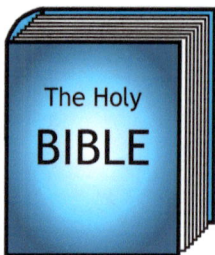

BIBLE

PRAY

FOOD

LIZARD

BED TIME

WHOLE BUNCH

THANKFUL

FLOWERS

TIME

FAMILY

FRIENDS

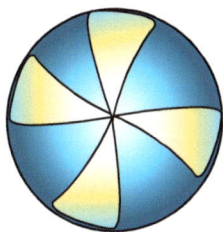 NEW BALL	 MOMMY	 DADDY
 GOD LOVES YOU	 BAD THINGS	 HANDS
 LOVED ONE	 APPLES	 PRAY FOR THEM
 ASK GOD	 SCARED	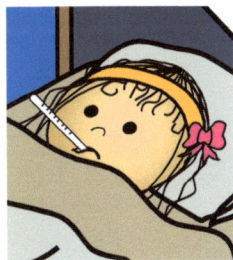 SICK

God Really Loves You Book Series™

GodReallyLovesYou.com

Matthew 6:9-15 After this manner therefore pray ye: Our Father which art in heaven, Hallowed be thy name. 10 Thy kingdom come. Thy will be done in earth, as it is in heaven. 11 Give us this day our daily bread. 12 And forgive us our debts, as we forgive our debtors. 13 And lead us not into temptation, but deliver us from evil: For thine is the kingdom, and the power, and the glory, for ever. Amen. 14 For if ye forgive men their trespasses, your heavenly Father will also forgive you: 15 But if ye forgive not men their trespasses, neither will your Father forgive your trespasses.

Matthew 18:3-5 And said, Verily I say unto you, Except ye be converted, and become as little children, ye shall not enter into the kingdom of heaven. Whosoever therefore shall humble himself as this little child, the same is greatest in the kingdom of heaven. And whoso shall receive one such little child in my name receiveth me.